Bedwyr Williams
The Gulch

Barbican

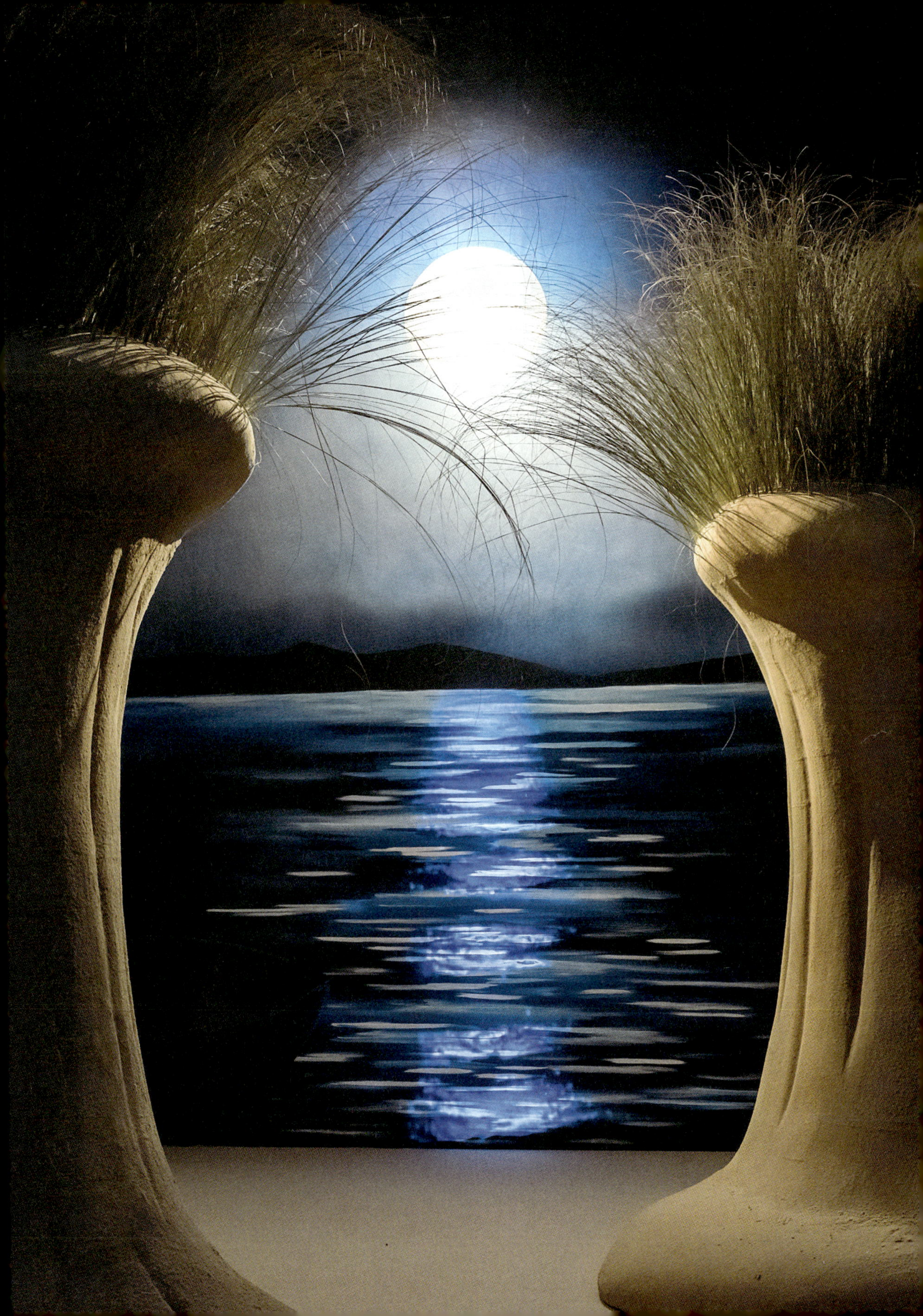

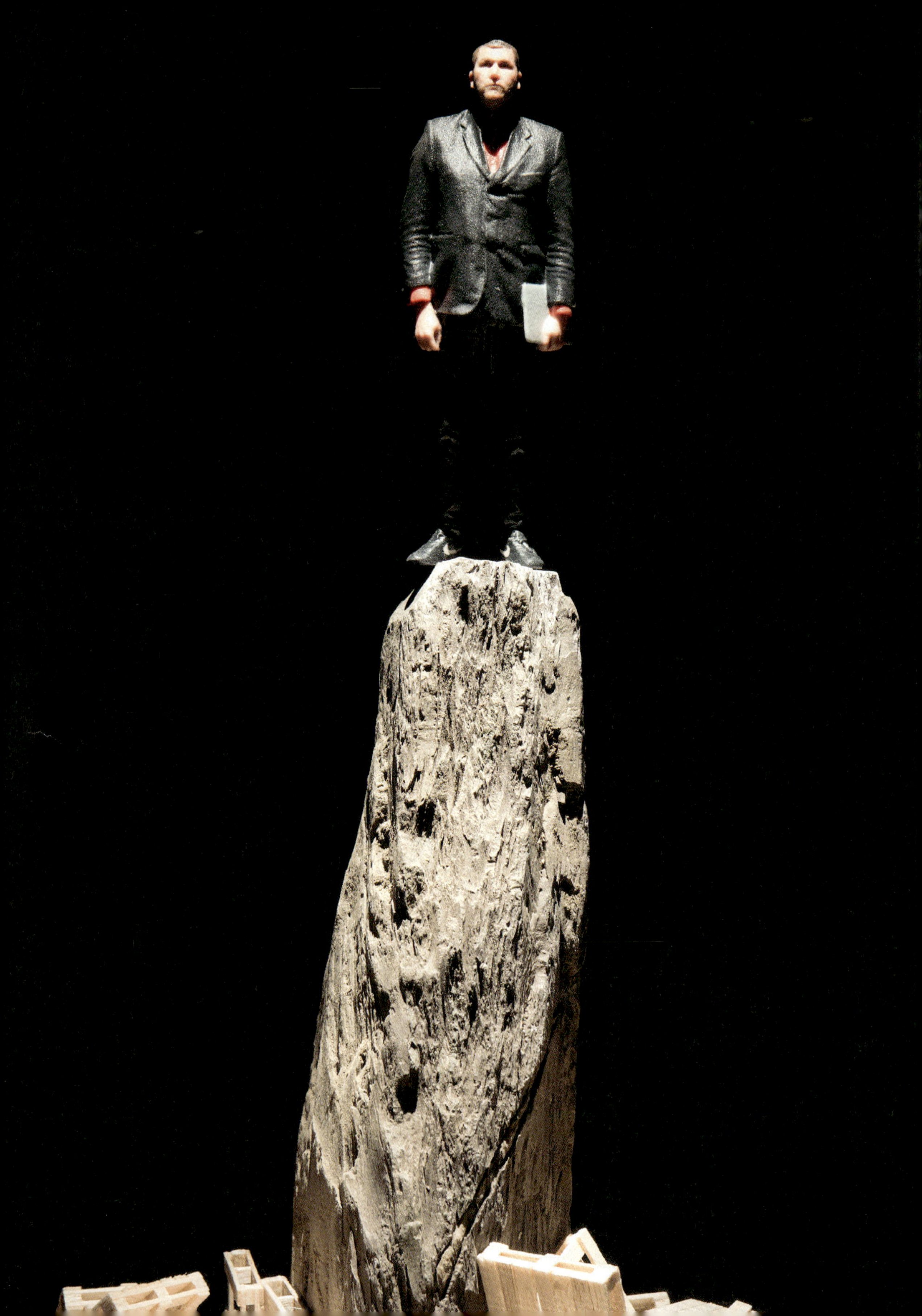

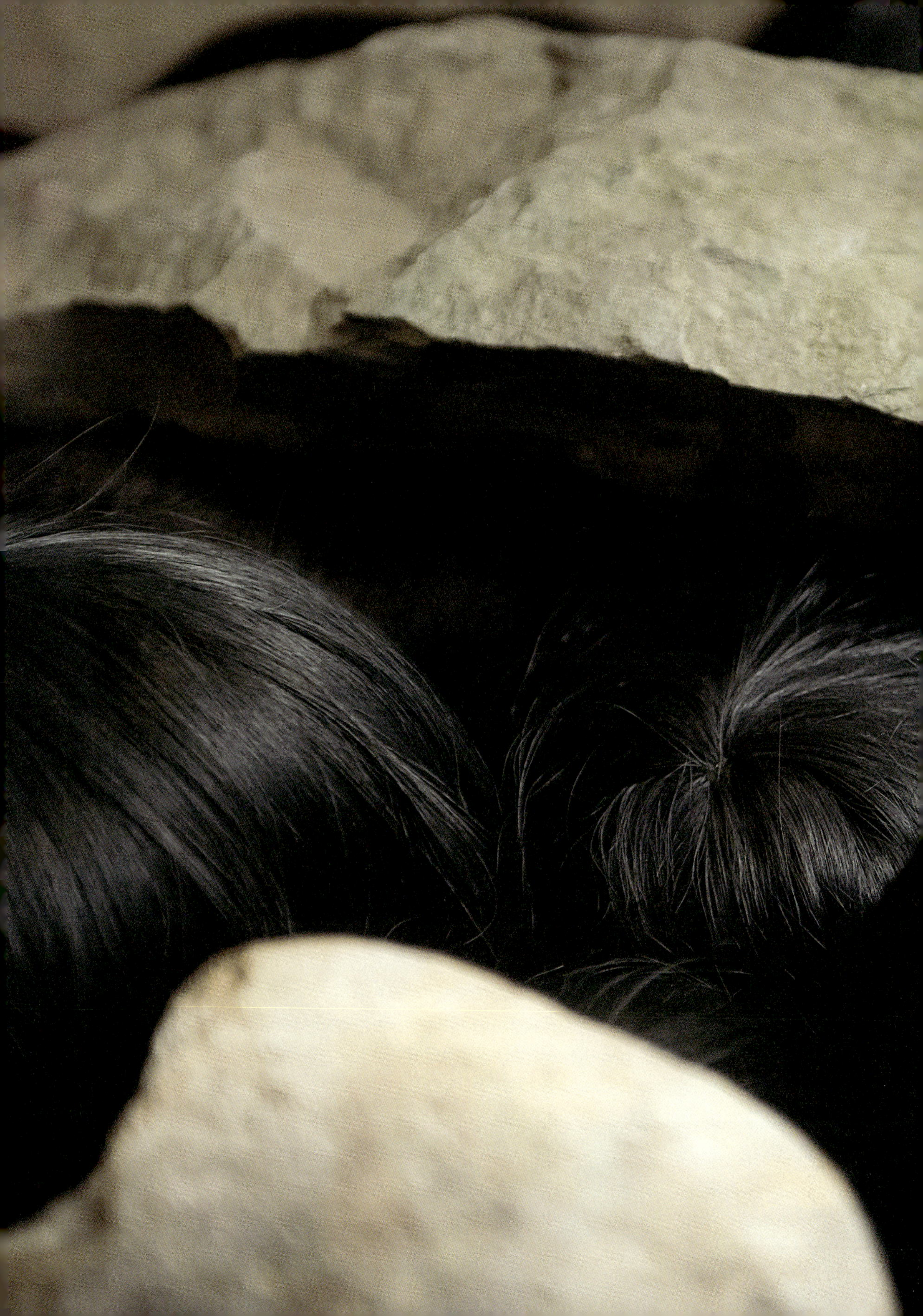

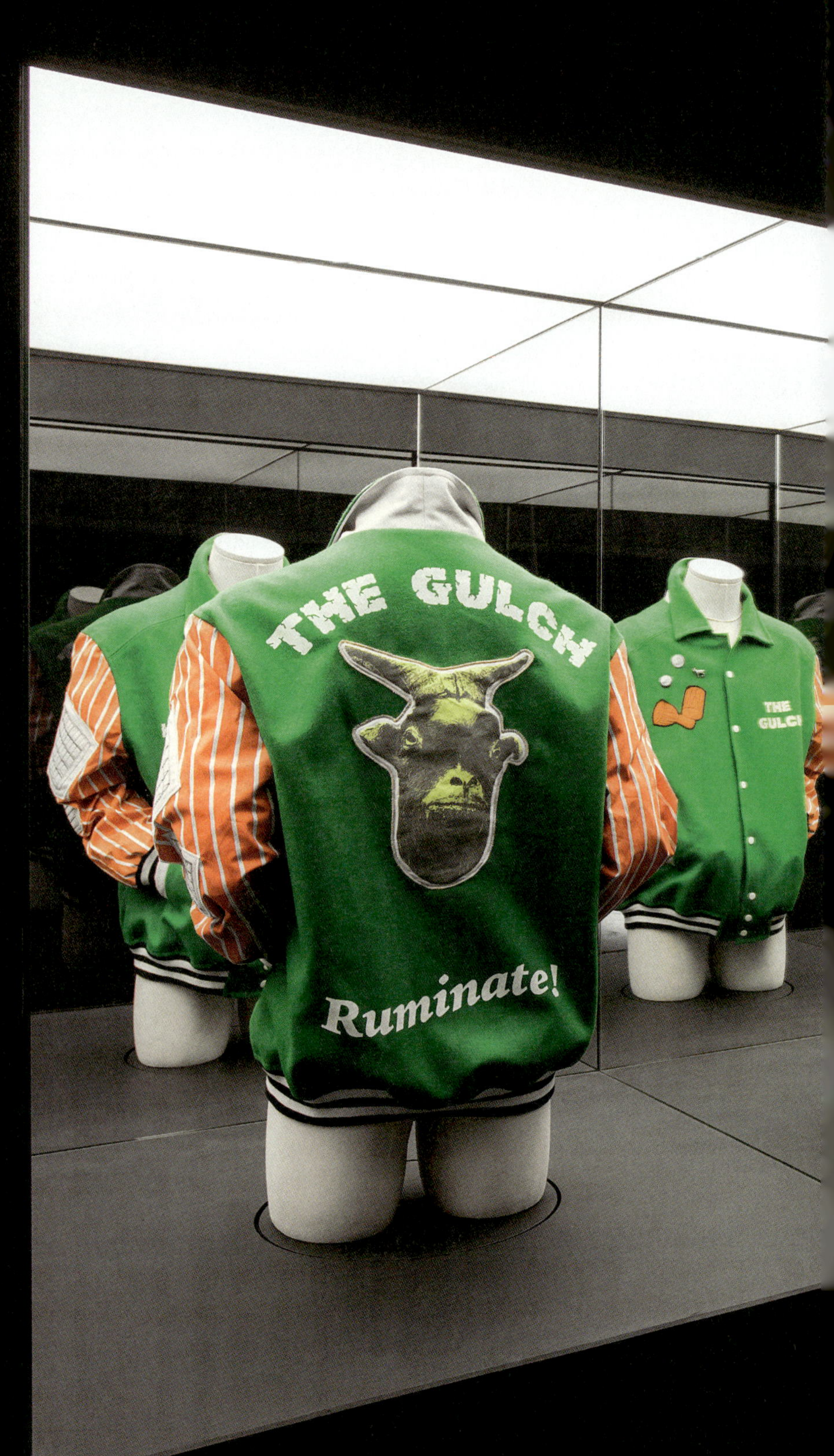
THE GULCH
Ruminate!
THE GULCH

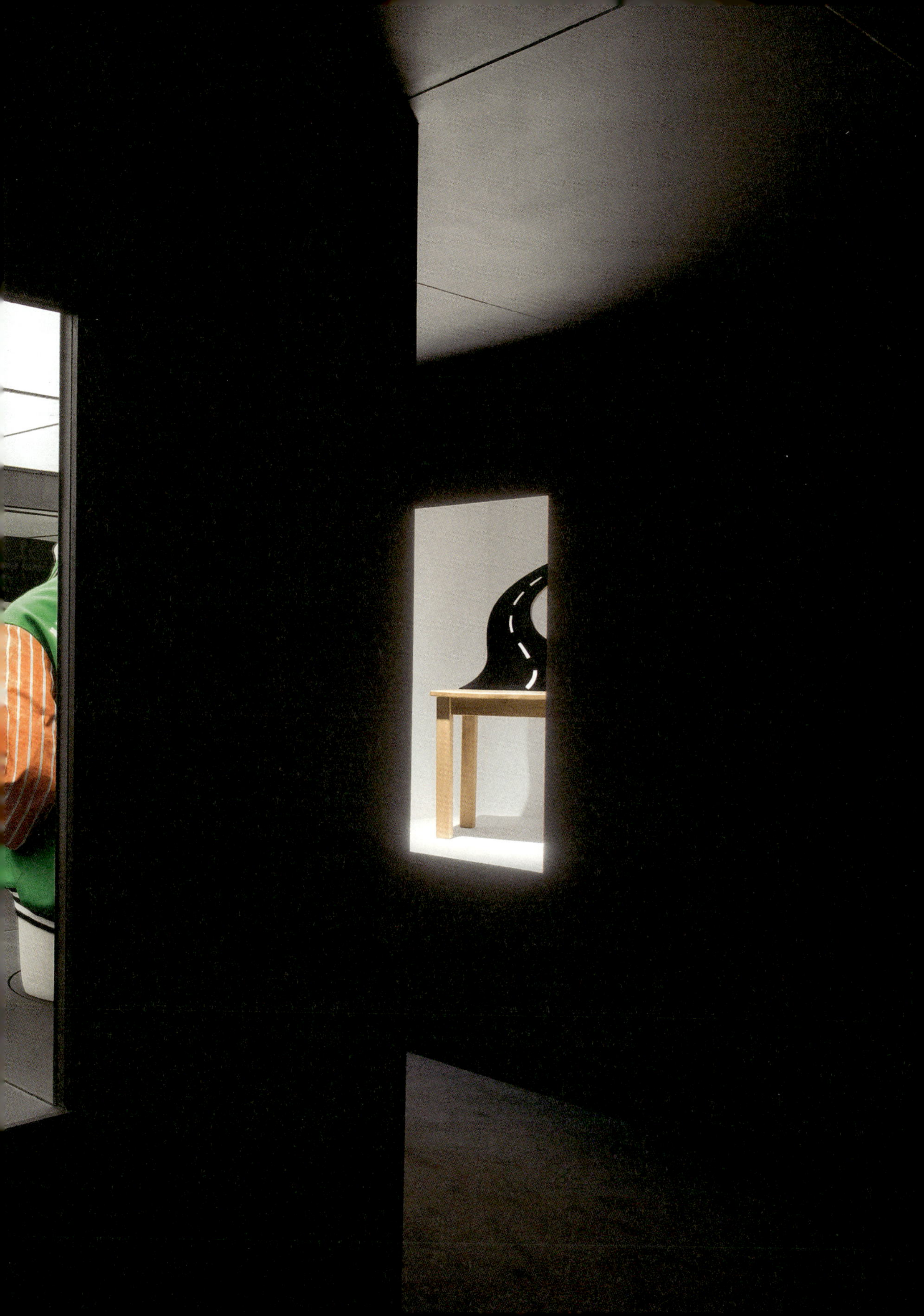

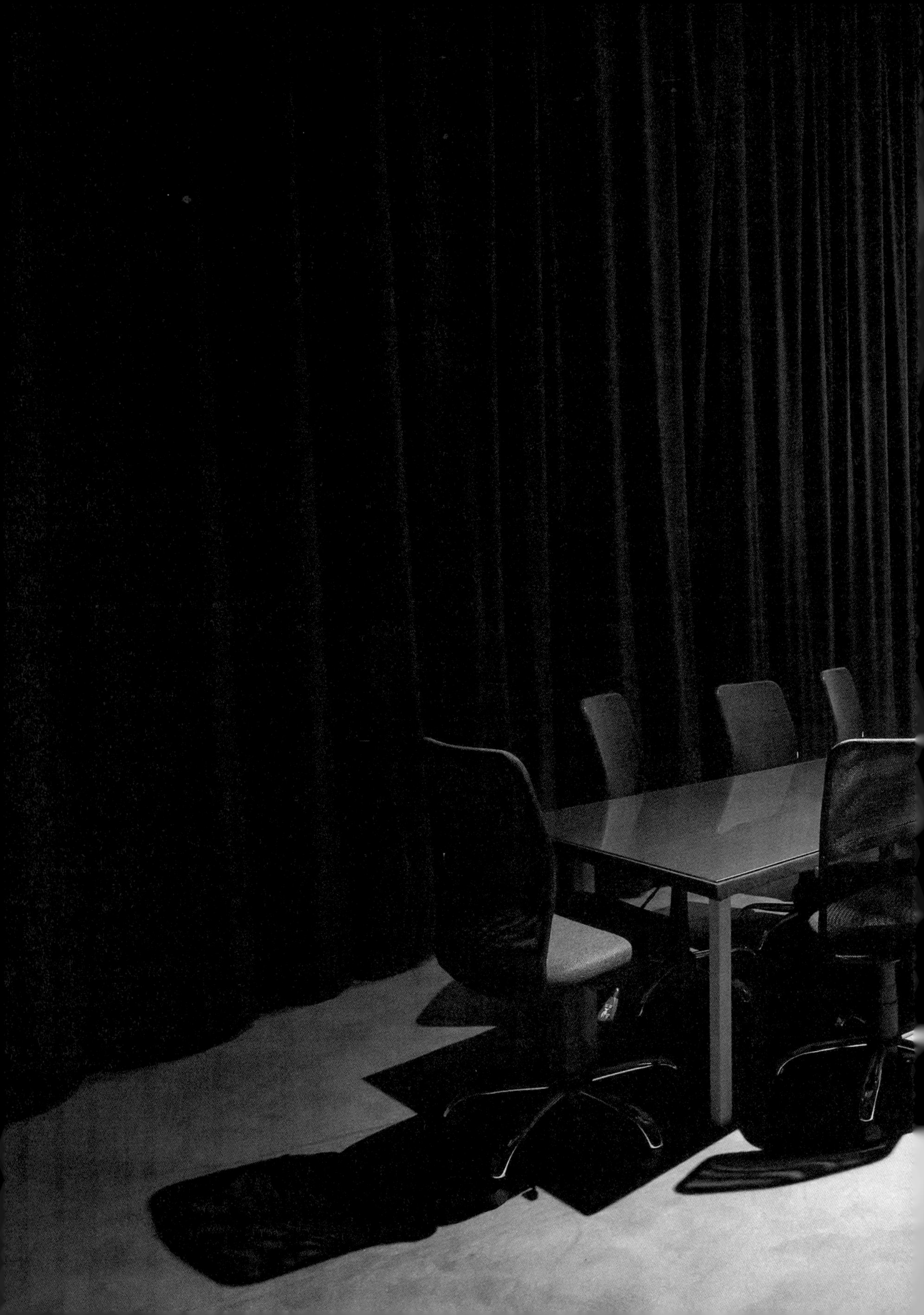

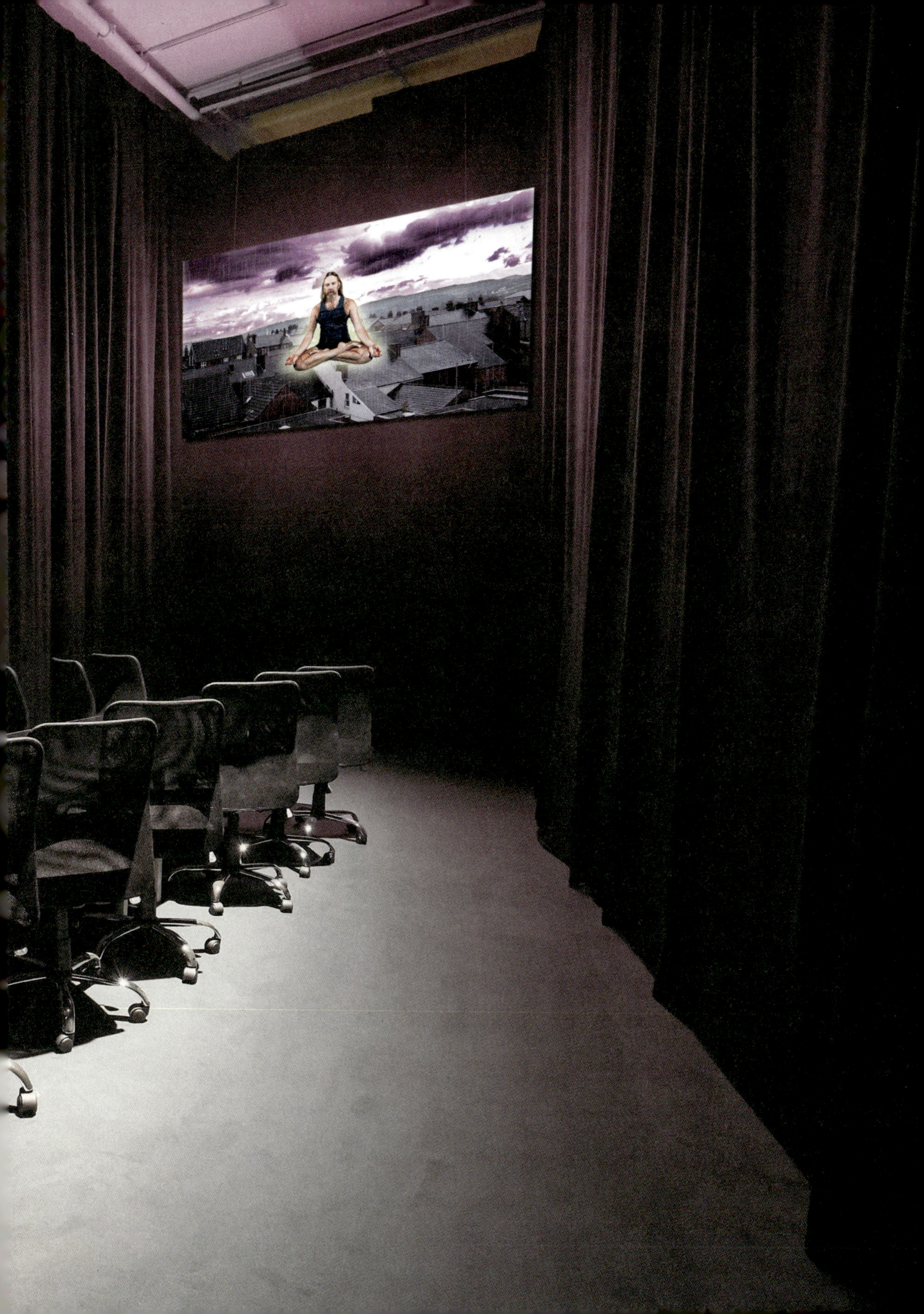

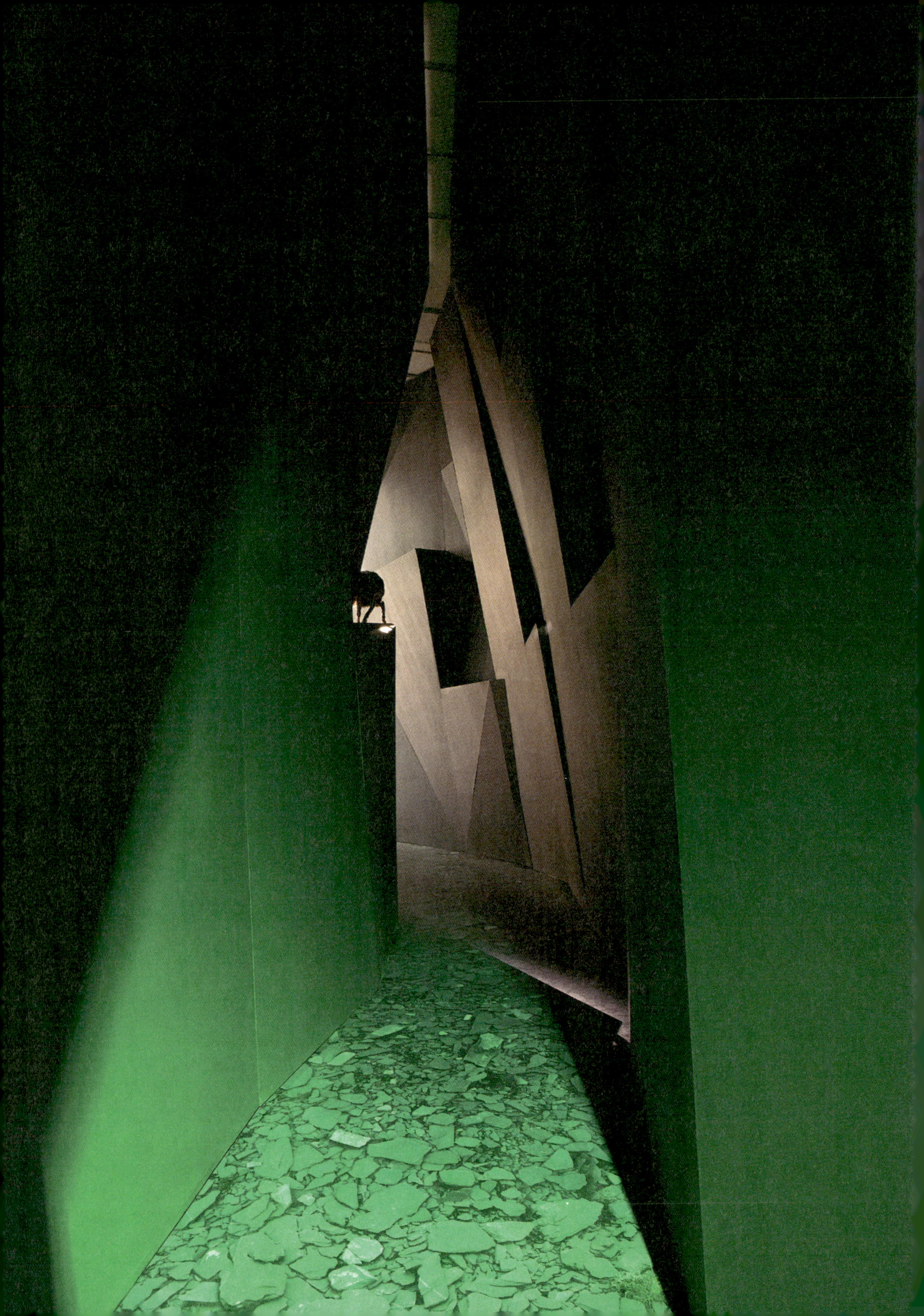

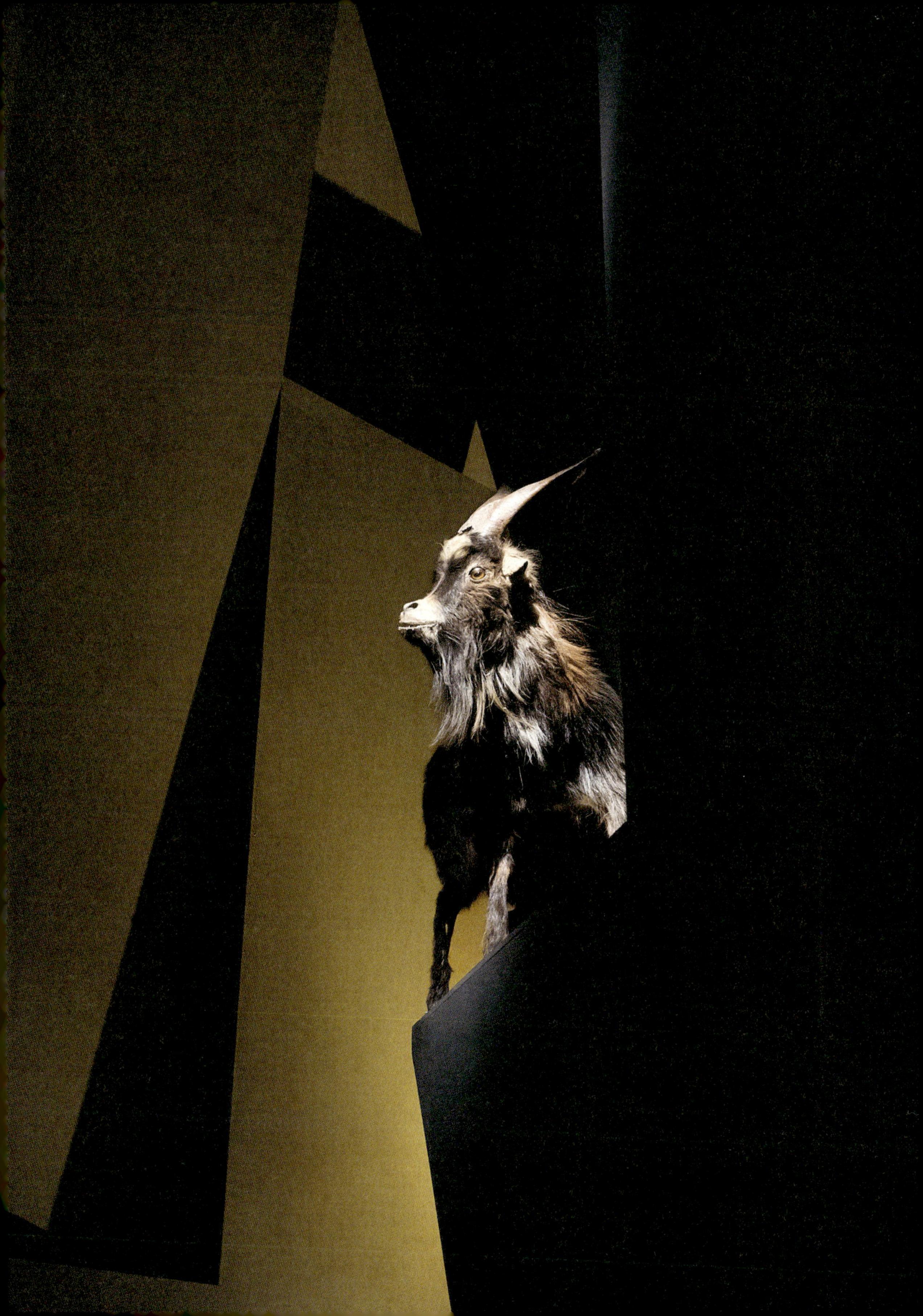

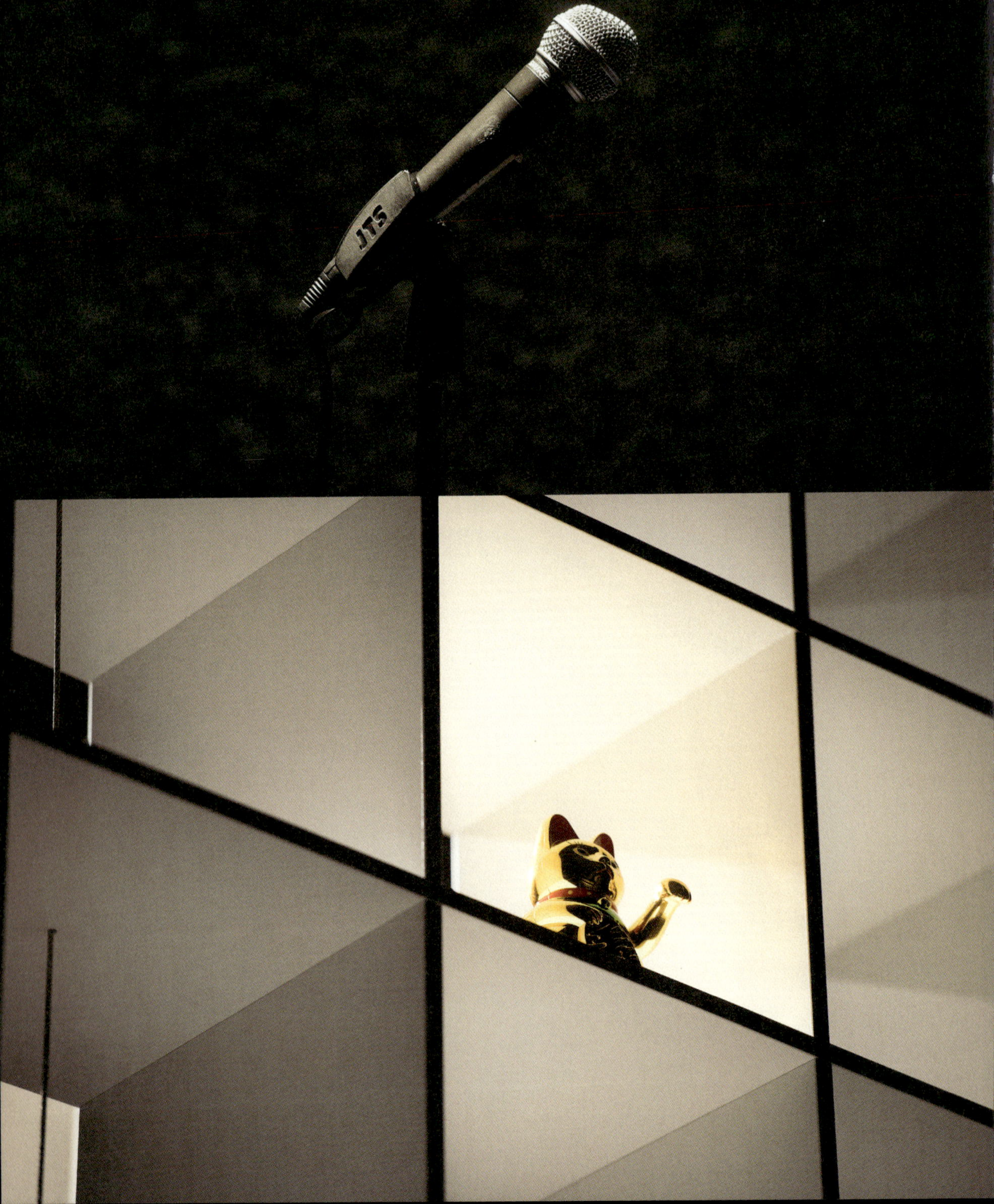

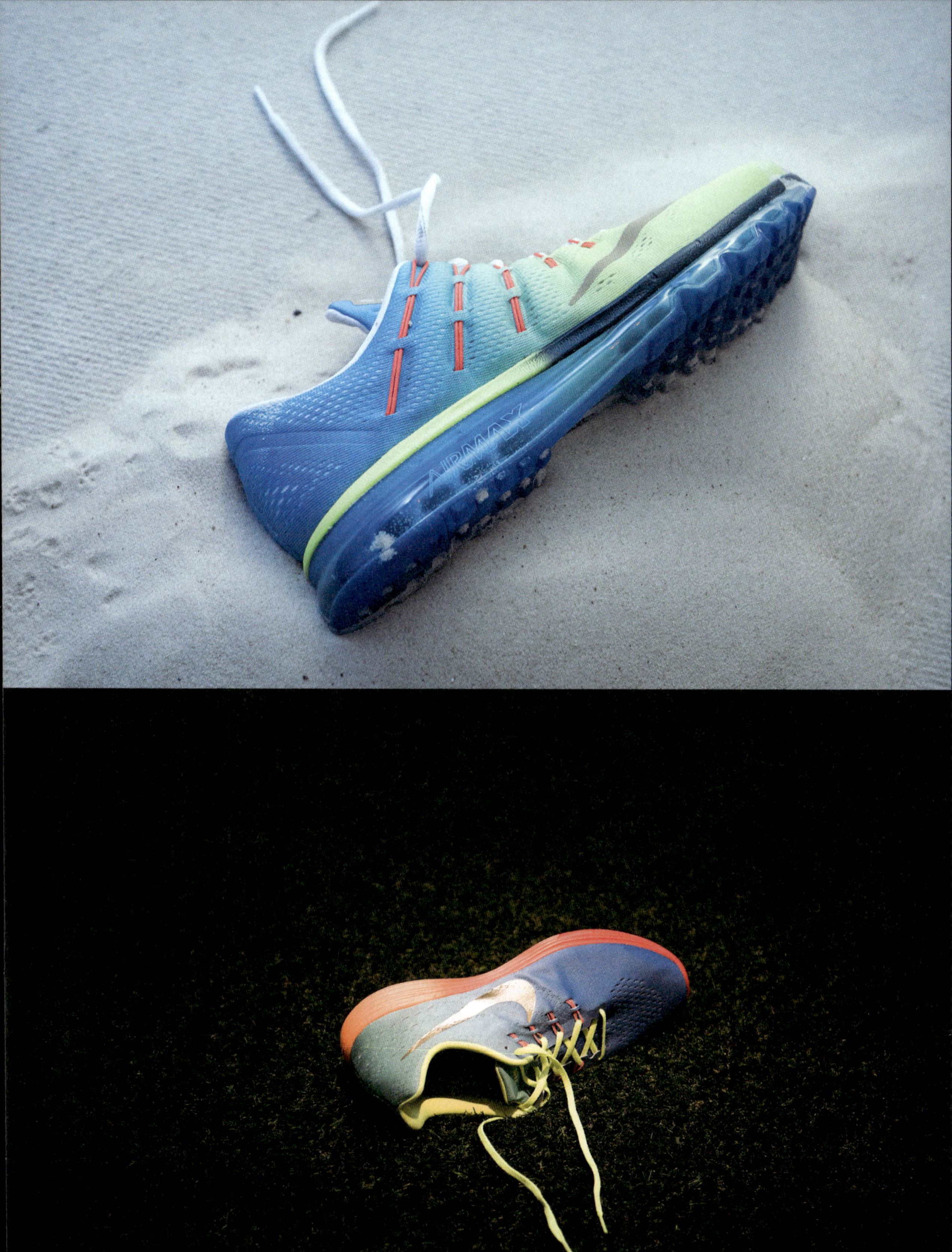

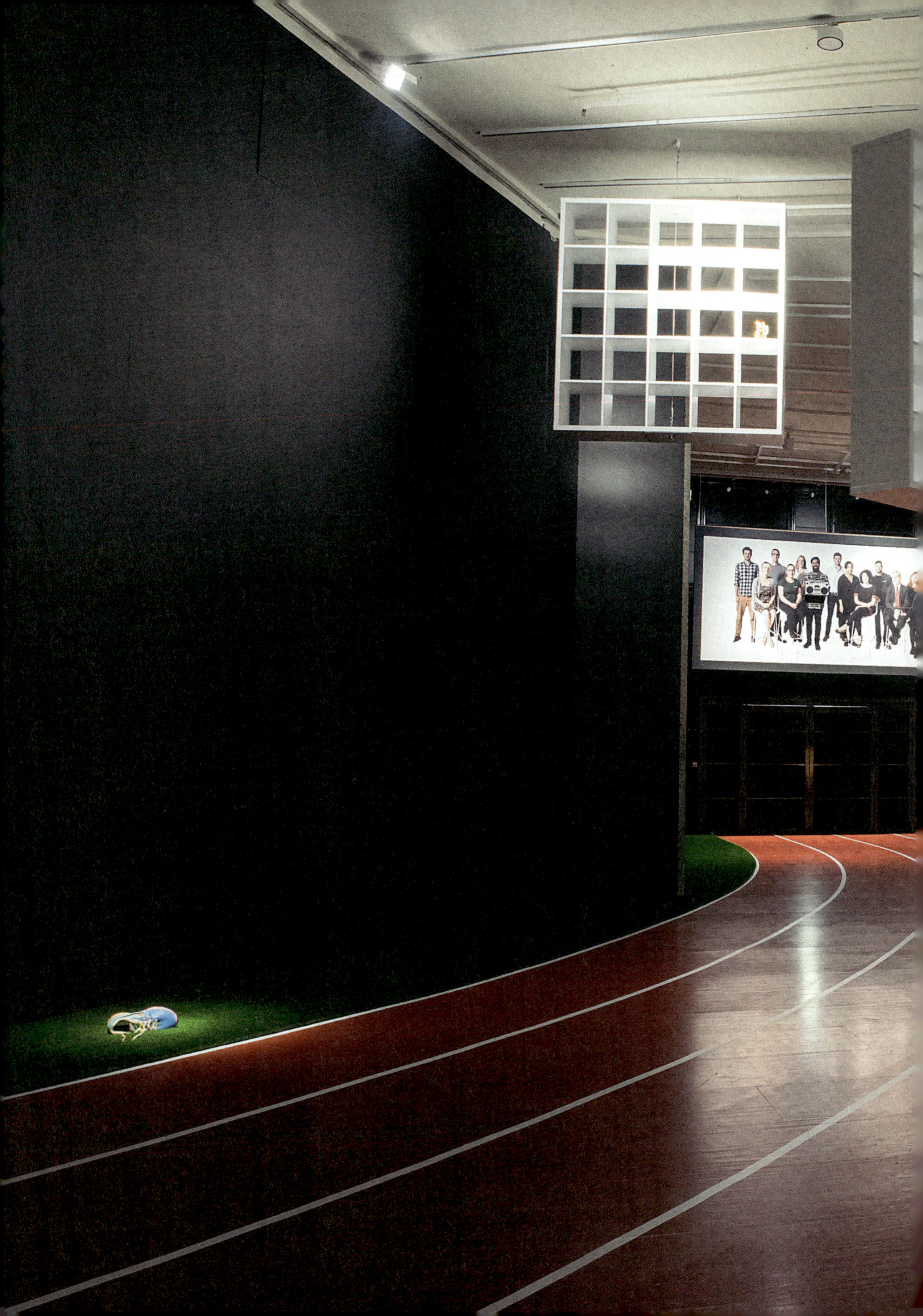

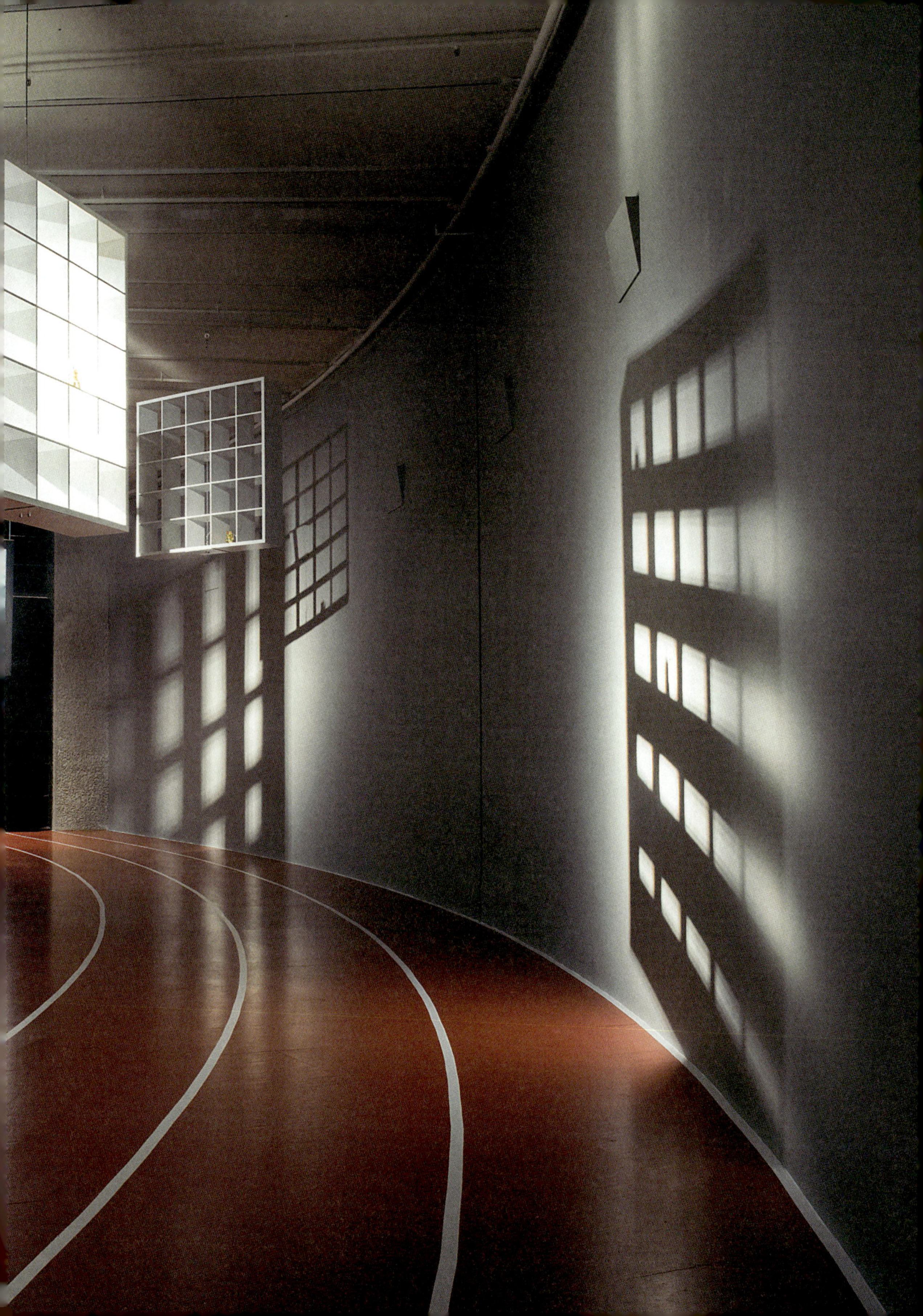

Ruminations on a Ledge
Sally O'Reilly

I like to jump about. I like to climb. To enquire. I'm inquisitive.
I want to see. Hear. Smell. Taste. I buck and leap and climb and
jump and look and lick. Not just for the exercise. I want to know.
As much as one can know anything these days. And I like to
want. I enjoy wanting like I enjoy a good stretch. Needing is something I don't enjoy. That's a push – not a stretch. It's a different
sort of leap that comes from needing. My leaps are luxuries,
I grant you that. Some among us are penned in. I feel for them
when I buck and leap and climb and jump and look and lick.
Because life is movement. Our core must keep moving for us
to be alive.

It's no wonder I'm constantly hungry, with all this moving
and climbing and wanting and leaping and licking. They say I'm
omnivorous, an eating machine. They use me for land clearance.
But this is a gross garbling of my motivations. I'm game, certainly.
I'll give anything a go. And if I do swallow something rum, one
of my four stomachs can usually deal with it. But in actual fact,
I'm really quite discerning. There are certain things that meet
my requirements. Certain things that are to my taste. They nour-
ish me. Everything else is potential. Or roughage. To be passed
through as a mistake. To be avoided next time. If I can remember.

It may surprise you that I have a repertoire. An unexpected
sophistication, when I appear so lawless. But I'm neither nihilistic
nor rule-bound. My knowledge is rigorous, yet I'm not fixed on it.
I will suck anything to see. In fact, I'll try anything twice – the first
time to find out, the second time to make sure. And I'll have
a third go too, if I feel like it. I ceaselessly sample this and that.
Then the other that. I never exhaust the possibilities. Because
what looks the same as something else could well be made up of
a totally different past. Its flavour might be all its own because
of where it's been, who else it's passed through, where it's
going next. Every nibble is unique. Every swallow an event without precedence. Every turd an artefact of a specific time and
place. Histories are chronicled in dung. It's my task to make those

histories mixed and multiple. Representative. Slurry can be rearranged any number of ways and it will still be slurry. My turds are like diamonds: individual immutable truths, traceable to the source material that inspired them.

So you can begin to understand, I hope. I'm sensitive. I mourn the constant loss of memories. I run and leap and climb from them. I rehearse the future. Ideas carry me onwards. An idea is a project in its most compressed form. And as a project unfolds, so does the future. Projection is the best mode of existence. Over there. I'm aiming over there. I make my way there by a series of leaps that I've rehearsed over a lifetime in infinite permutations. I jump about in search of my future self. I climb to see better, and to be better seen. I buck for attention, which I crave. And yet I wish to be at a remove. Aloft. I am a paradox. A half-and-half. Two-faced. Shit-faced and sober-minded. Looking and leaping. Forwards and back.

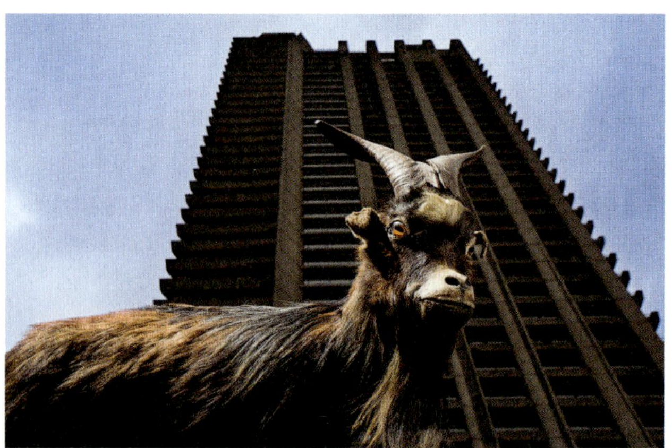

Naturally, I look before I leap, although it may not seem like it to an onlooker. I appear casual. Capricious. These are the same people who will say that I have a wicked eye. But they're paranoid fabulists. They're seeking connections that don't exist. Yes, my pupils are rectangular, oriented along the horizontal. And no, I don't have the blind spot of other mammals, whose eyes have not yet adapted to being on either side of their face. My field of vision encompasses 320 degrees. Nearly the full circle. But does this make me evil? Is it not said that the gods are all-seeing? That makes me closer to the gods than you. The devil take you, if he can find you. I will always be able to see you.

Your paranoia and my creativity overlap. Both require the making of connections beyond the blindingly obvious. Is that

Goat from The Gulch, 2016. Ben Jonson Place, Barbican Centre, London. Photo: Max Colson.

not why we're both here? We're looking for the links, the leaps
that will make everything that much better. Let me guide you
through some leaps I've found. Let me help you leap from the
'what's to the 'how's, maybe. Many don't manage the 'why's or
the 'how's. They're stuck on the 'what's and the 'when's. They
want to know what this 'what' will be, which 'what' this 'how' will
make, when this 'then' will come, and how this 'that' will be.
They want their 'this's and 'and's guaranteed, their 'that's and
'then's on time. But there are others who prefer to be surprised.
To not know what's coming. To be unable to recognise what it
is when it's arrived. I like to think of you as one of these. I like
to imagine that you know that knowing is banal or corporate
or impossible. I hope you never find out. Mystery is life. Death
is knowledge. Guessing is more fun.

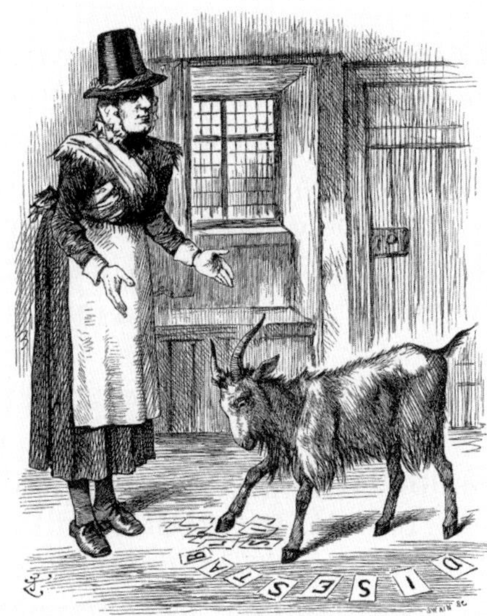

THE LEARNED WELSH GOAT.

So you stand and stare at me. In fact, lots of men stare
at me. I don't know why. I'm more like them than they realise.
Armies use my cadaver for medical training. Our bodies are that
similar. (Our minds less so.) I too have two teats and a beard,
which some might think contradictory. My two teats bring forth a
musky, frothing milk that even the intolerant can swallow. And
what is it that men's breasts bring forth? Hubris. And women's?
Hubris and milk. You upright, furless agents of quick change.
You recognise our bodies as similar to your own, and yet see it
only for its material qualities. You feel no compunction at using

our innards for catgut. You bow and pluck our guts in anthems and ballads that celebrate your greatness and your lost loves. You sew up your own wounds with our gizzards. You shave us, humiliate us, then cover your own shameful nakedness with our exquisite cashmere coat.

But there is a part of us that humans do not value. It is the part that we value most ourselves. We learned early on that if we wished what we hold dear to remain in our possession, then we should learn to love what no one else can. Our smell is glorious. Higher than your domes and spires. We may lend its edge to the cheeses that you press upon your vegetarians, but you will never let it hang raw in your delicate nostrils. You sedate your convicts with what you call our stench. You demonise us for it. But your mephitis is my Spanish fly. My love pisses on his forelegs and his own face when it is our time. What a feat. What gallantry. I am wild for it.

Yes – wild. I may seem domesticated, but I still have the ancient, horny, audacious drives. My thoughts scatter like panic. My ramblings are heretic. I rock your rationalism. I make pagan farces of your pious techno-logic. I whisper obscenities into the ears of your saints. Satanism would be going too far, granted. I don't want to scare the fluids out of you, merely to jolt you into new thoughts. I don't put new and noxious notions into your head. I stir what's already there into novel connection. I leap from one familiar idea to another, to show you quite how close they were all along. And now that you know, or have given up what you thought you knew, you can move on. We can want and move and live and smell together. We can eat together. Don't mind the stench. There might be something fruity in the middle. Give it a nibble. I'll lend you one of my stomachs. You can wash it down with my milk. We will digest the indigestible. Rub our scent along the way. Announce ourselves. Even those with the biggest blind spots can smell. They might get the drift. They might follow. Come on. Just a small leap. Over there. Then there. Then the next there…

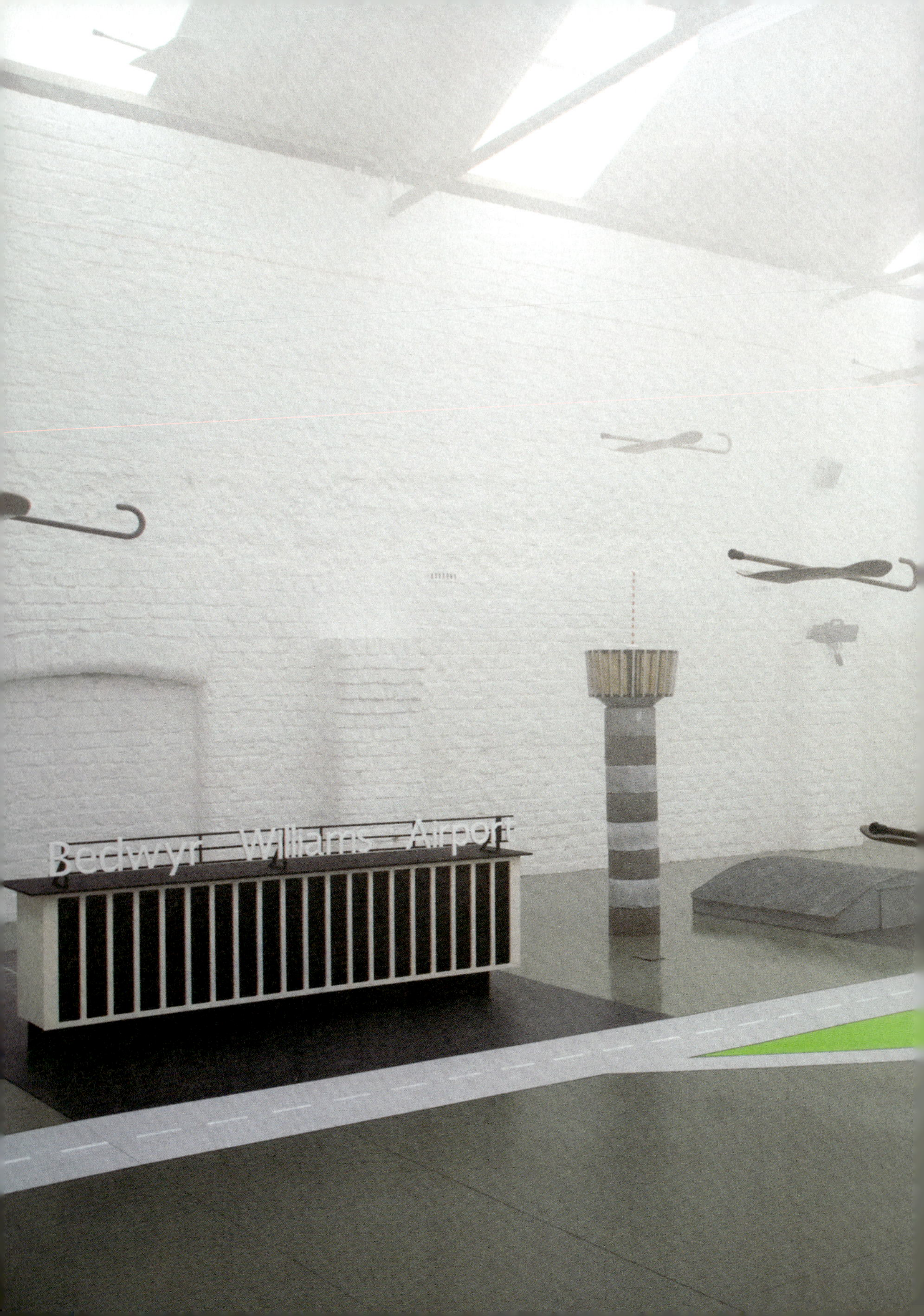

Bedwyr Williams Airport

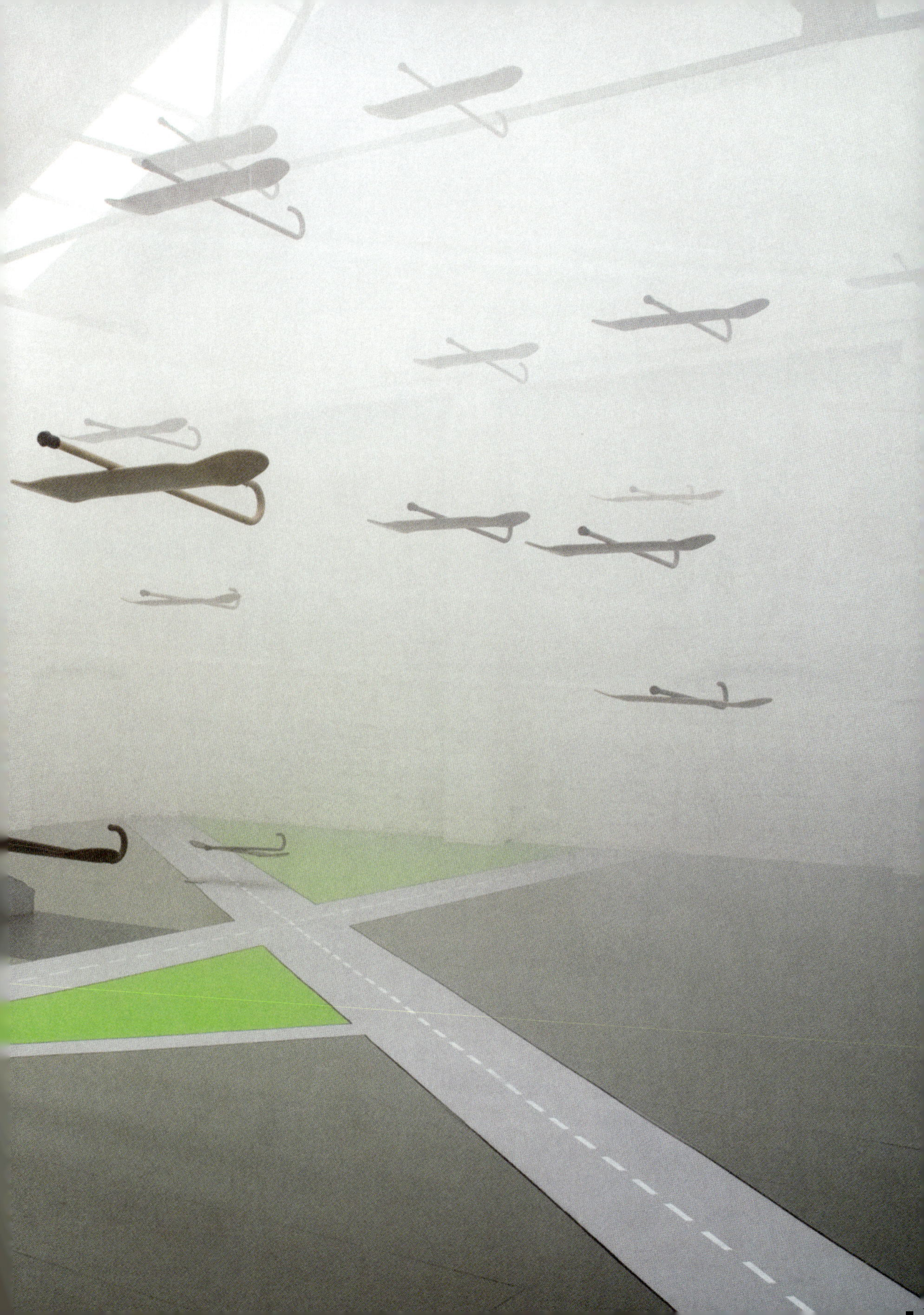

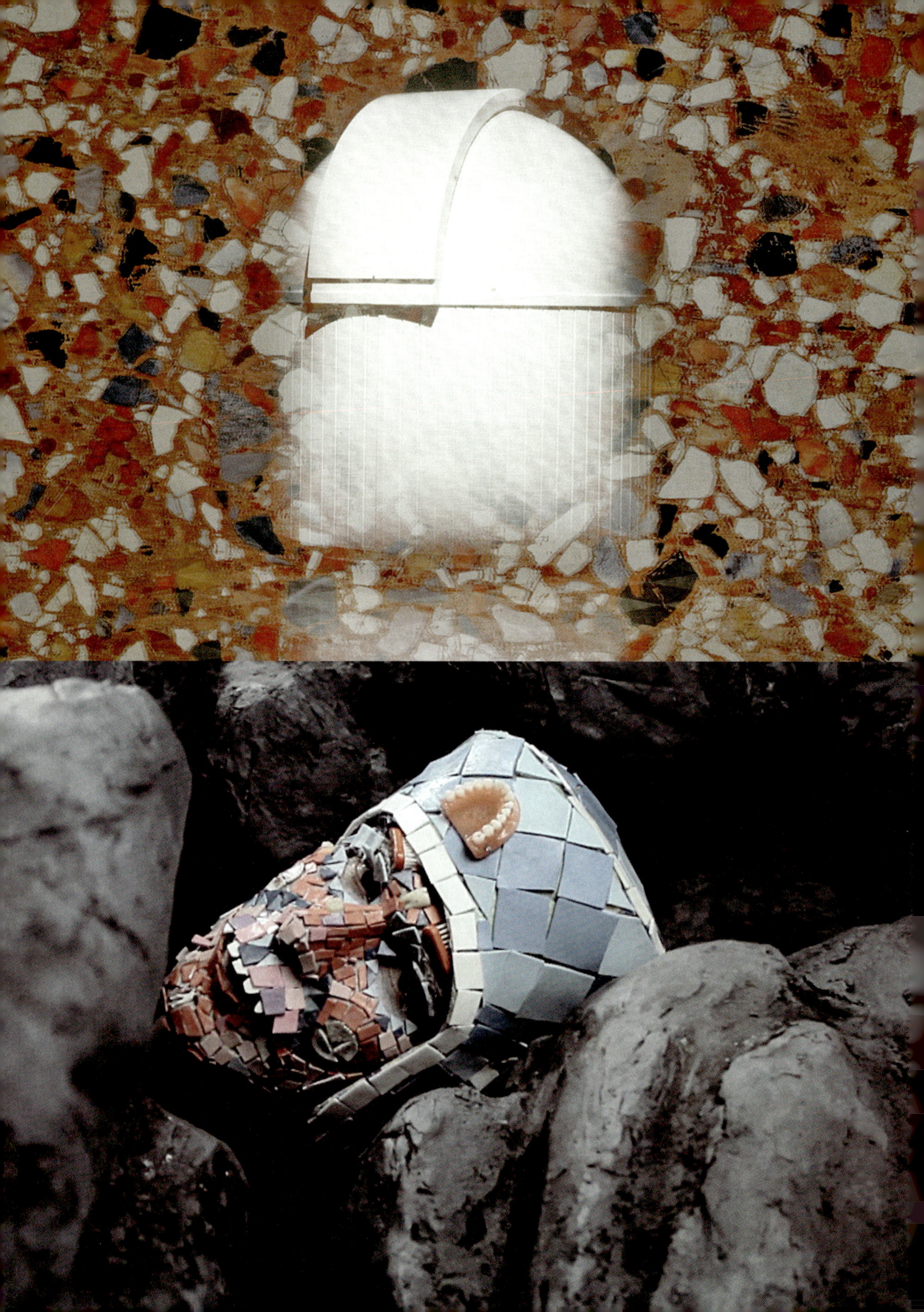

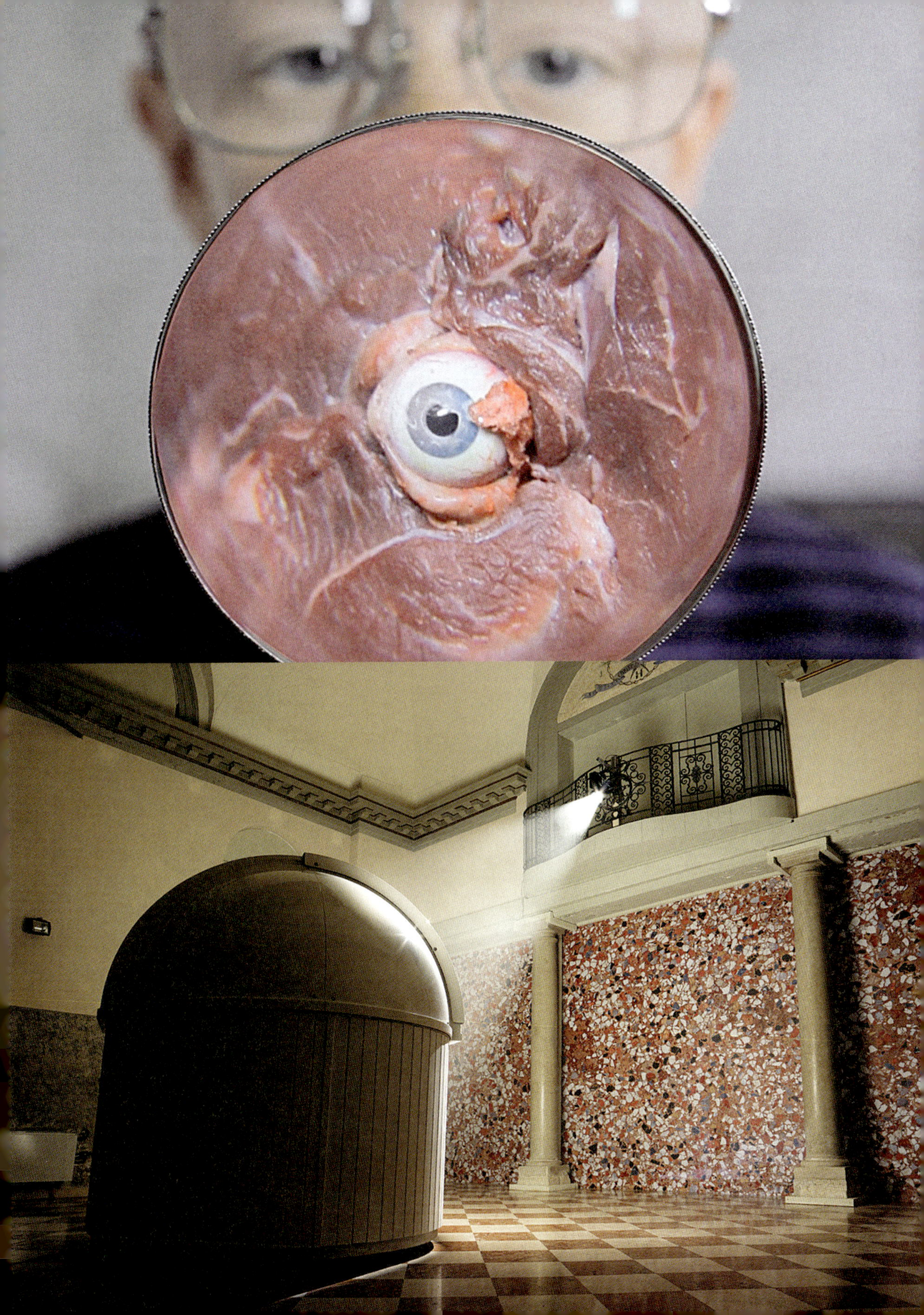

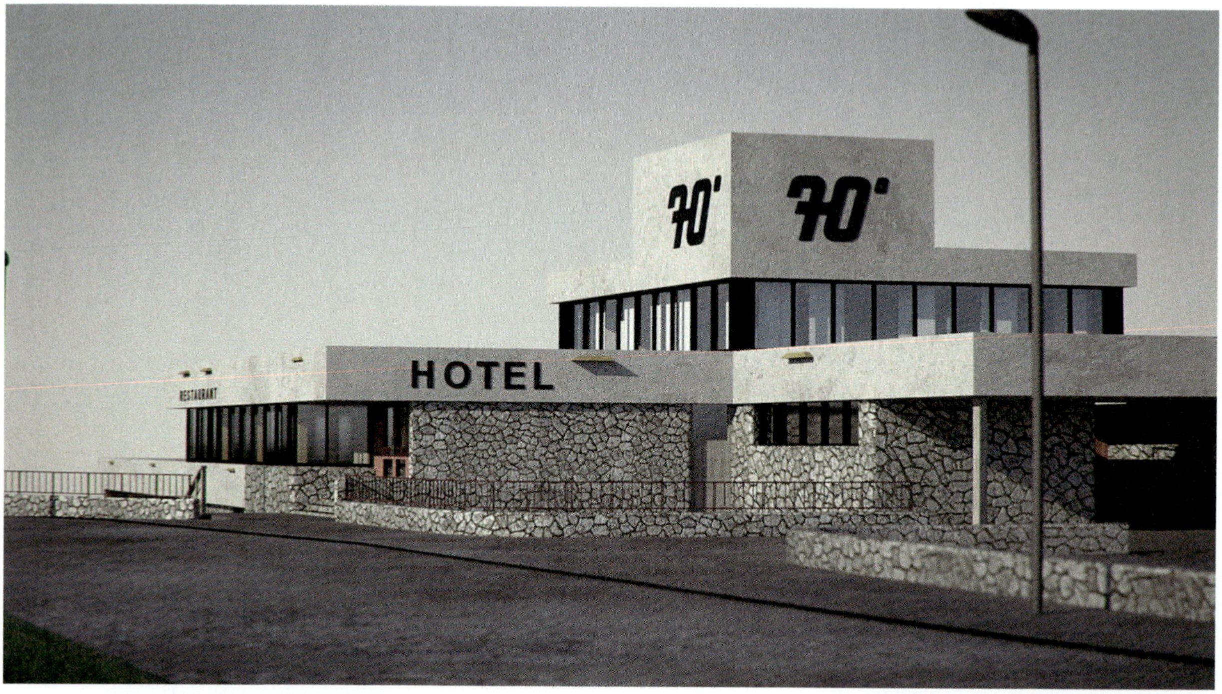

70'
70'
HOTEL
RESTAURANT

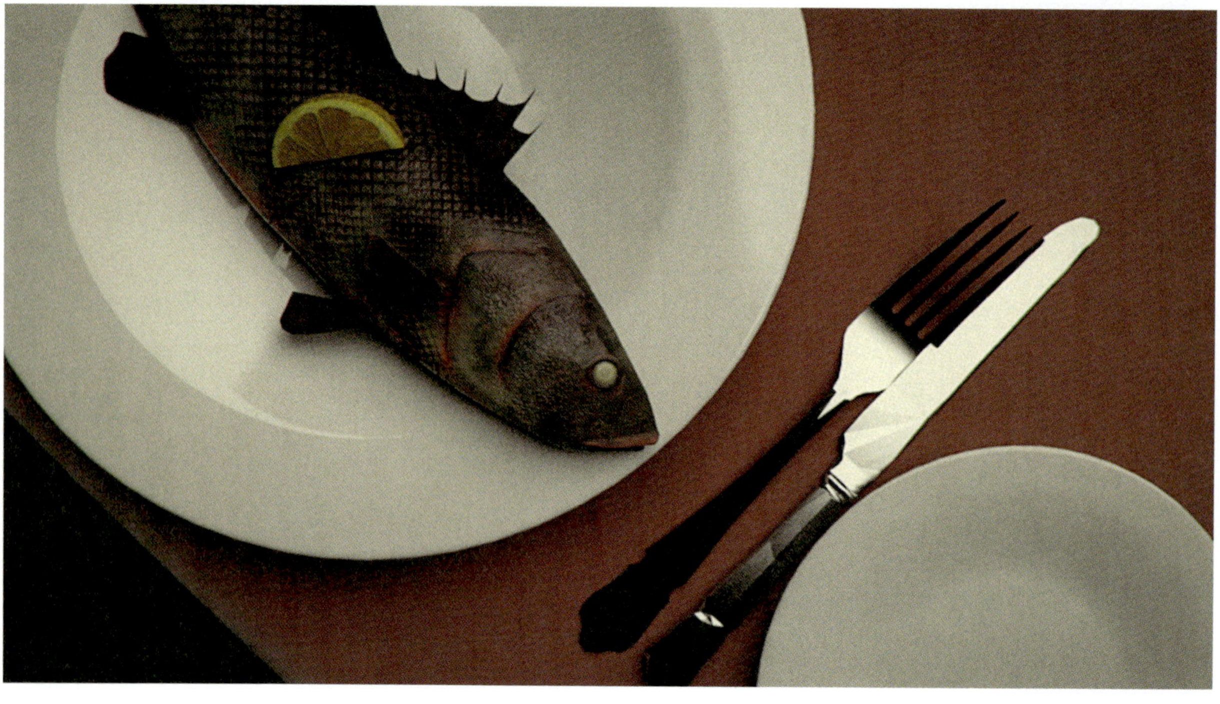

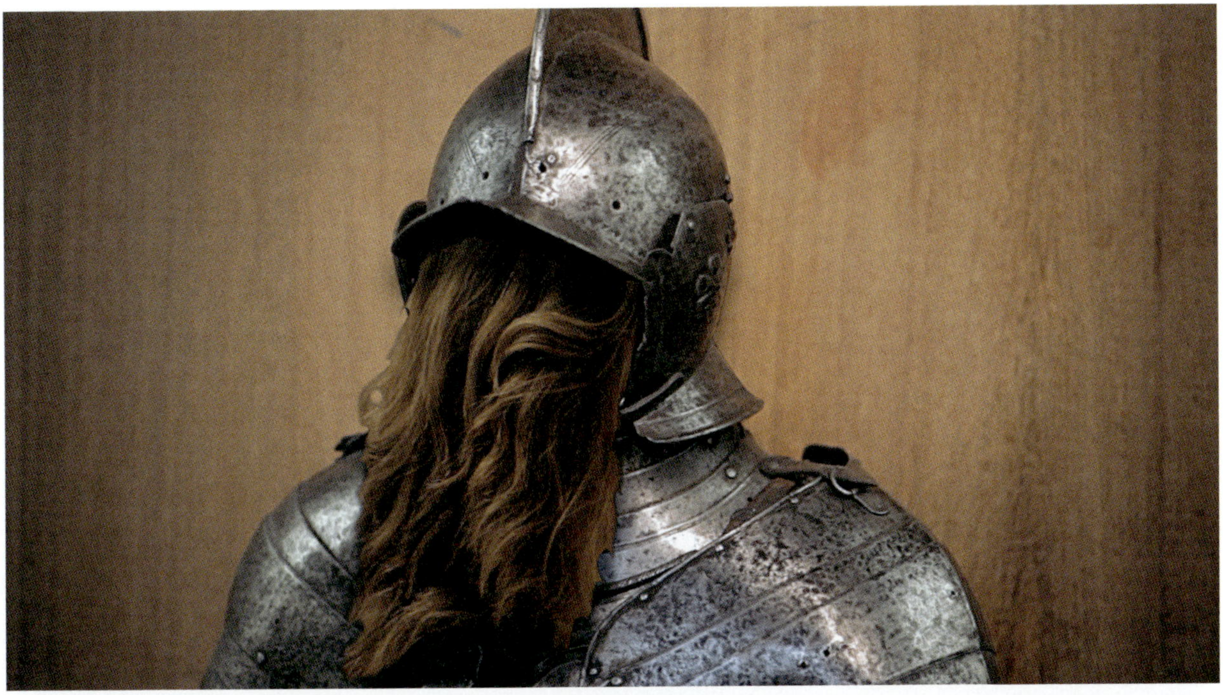

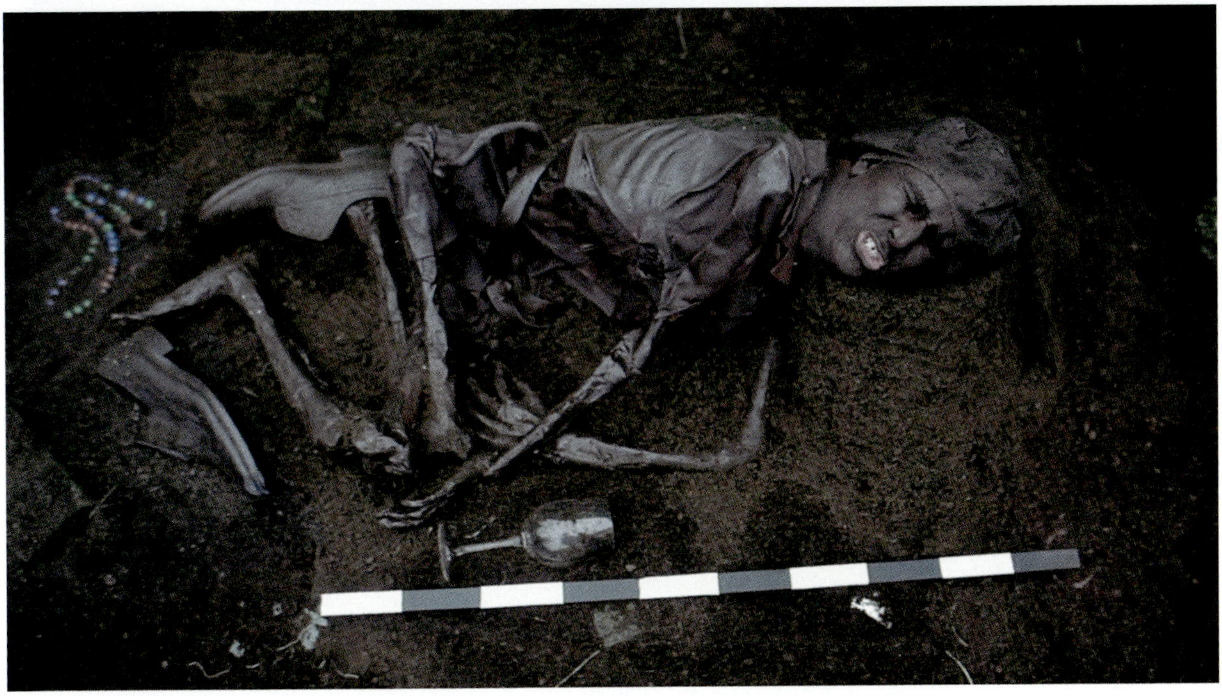

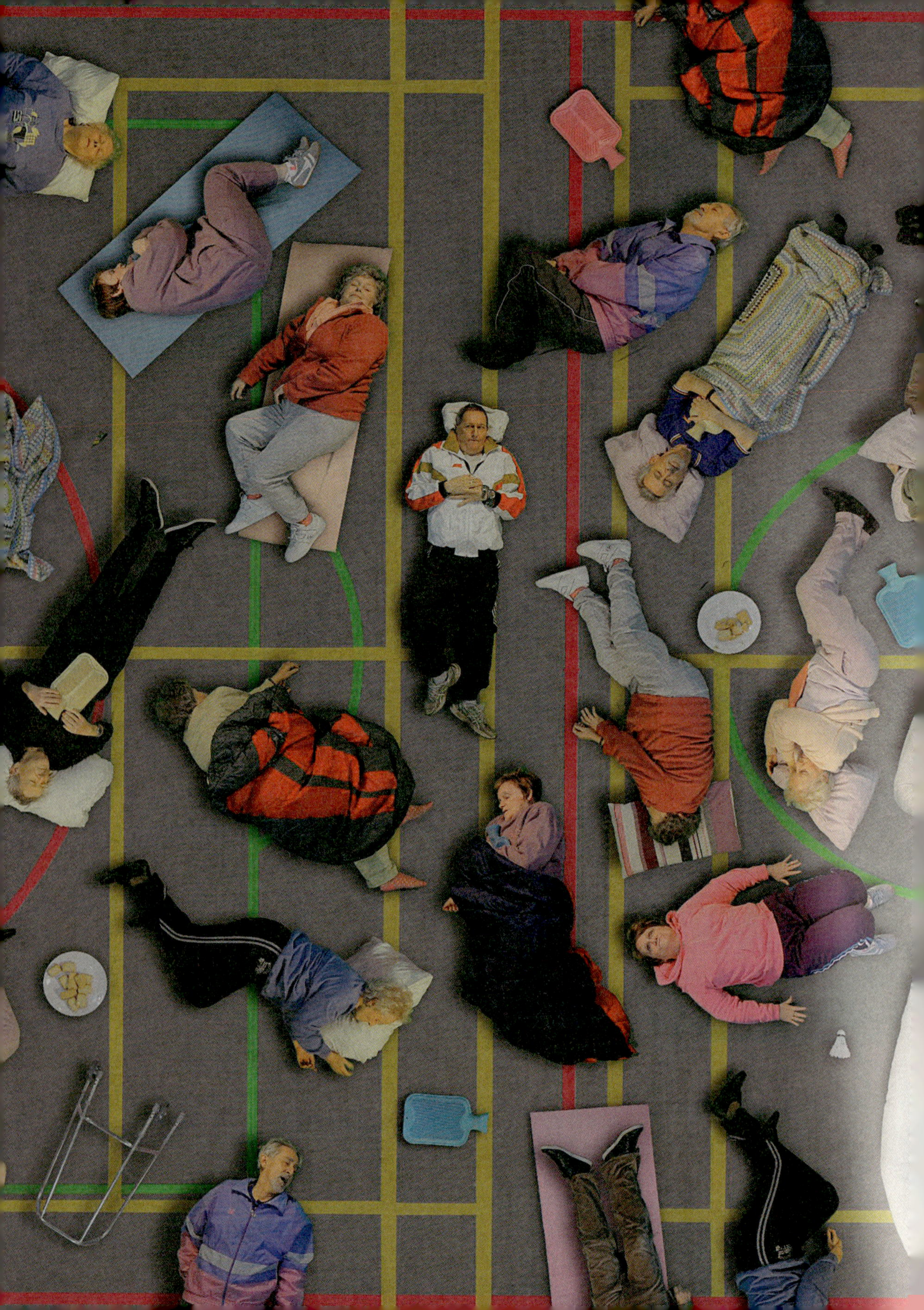

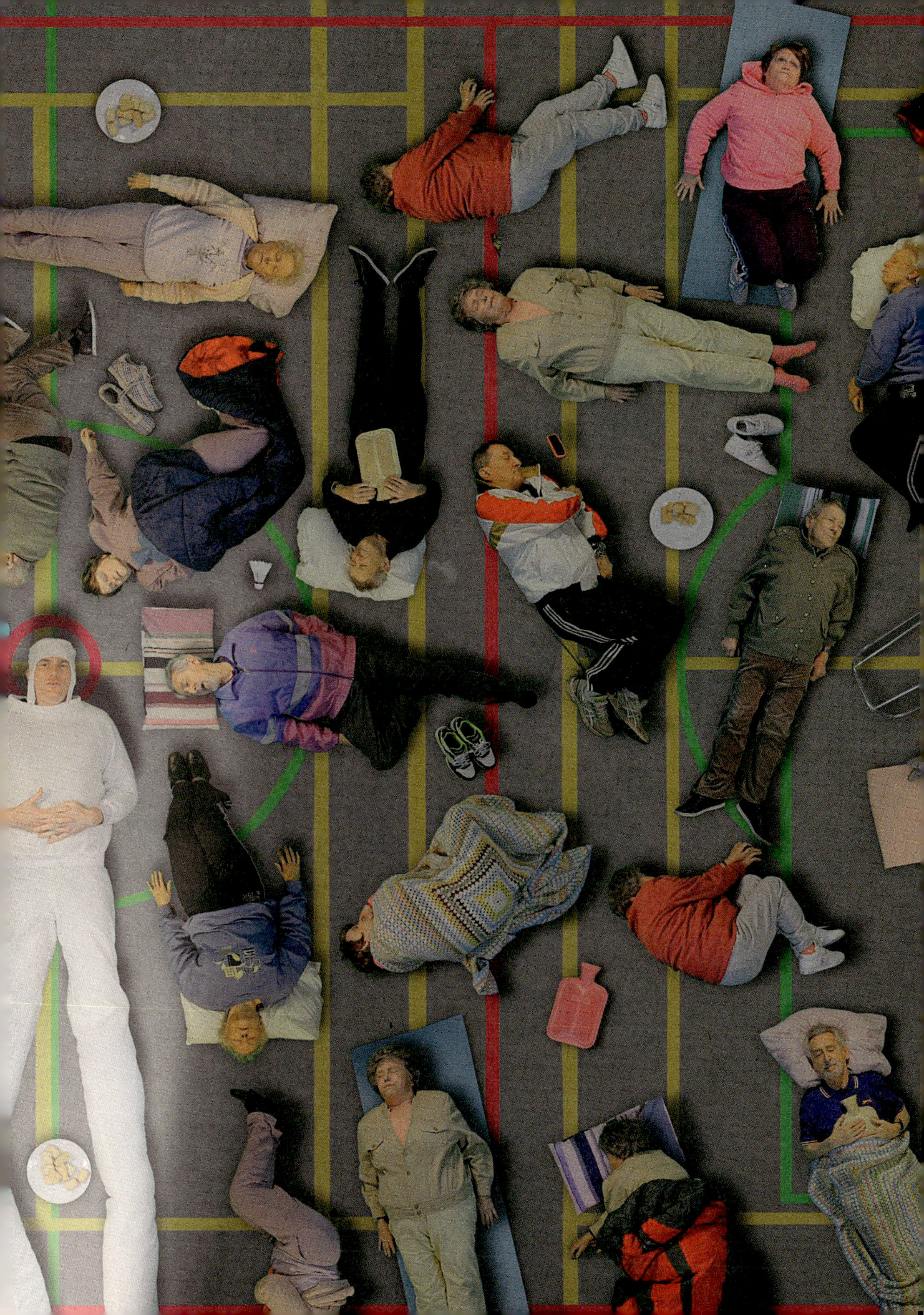

'I don't know whether to laugh or cry'
Bedwyr Williams in conversation with Lotte Johnson

LJ   Storytelling and performance are both an integral
        part of your practice. Your work has gained a
        more physical presence in recent years, taking
        the form of large-scale installations, but narratives
        or implied stories persist. Where did this interest
        come from?

BW   My grandfather was quite a raconteur. He would
        sit back after supper and tell stories about the
        past. I've also got memories of farming relatives
        who lived in houses that would look really alien
        today, really dark in the corners. The way that
        those people would share information – I loved
        listening to them. In 2003 I invented a Grim Reaper
        character and it was a real turning point. The
        spoken word aspect combined with some kind of
        visual prop – it's not stand-up comedy but it uses
        some of the same conventions.

LJ   I think you are right to push against that label
        because you're doing something quite different.
        I often think of your work in terms of satire,
        ridiculing the ways we grapple with social class,
        identity, our emotions.

BW   Yes, I'm probably more interested in satire than
     I am in comedy. I make work that's quite sarcastic,
     critical, or a bit acid in some of its views. At the
     same time as I don't consider my work comedy,
     I do like that 'because' thing. Someone asks 'why
     did you do it?' and the answer is just 'because'.
     It's something that a lot of Irish writers do so
     naturally, like James Joyce.

LJ   Samuel Beckett, too. I often think of Beckett in
     relation to your work and the idea of his 'theatre
     of the absurd': his tragicomic perspective on
     human existence, his irreverence, as well as his
     minimal but acute use of language.[1]

BW   Yes, Beckett absolutely. There's a really great
     TV adaptation of *Waiting for Godot* (1953).
     The set is brilliant – they've basically just got
     a load of quarry waste, put it in a round studio
     and painted the wall a sky-like colour. I've thought
     a lot about the Curve when looking at that.

LJ   What was it that specifically intrigued you about
     the Curve?

BW   When you come into it through those double doors
     you're standing at a weird point in the height of
     the space – you drop down into it, which is some-
     thing that's quite common in the Barbican.

There's a grotto feel to it. I particularly like
the idea of walking down to a beach at night,
and how atmospheric and enticing that could be,
with the sound of the sea lapping on the shore.
It's an alluring inky blue theatre set that sucks
you in. The Barbican is like that; it makes you
want to go into it.

LJ   When we first started talking about your com-
mission, you suggested creating an experience
like a ghost train, with a sense of embarking on
a journey.

BW   Definitely, I like the idea of disappearing
into something that's like a little diorama.
The sand dunes at the start of *The Gulch* are
also mysterious. Dunes are constantly collapsing
as well; there's something tragic about them.
Then there's the running shoe… There's a story
of people's feet that have been washing up on
the beach in Canada. The running shoe preserves
the foot, even as the rest of the body gets
nibbled away. A right foot in a size 11 Nike;
it's a beautiful but gruesome image. When you
see something like that you try to imagine the
person who lost it.

LJ   Then you imagine what's happened to its other
half.

BW Was it a sad situation? Will they miss each other? You think about all the stuff you have lost yourself. The things that wash up on the beach stink too. The sea is amazing but filthy – even without all of the crap that we put into it, it's kind of a disgusting thing.

LJ It's almost the bowel of the earth, verging on lewd.

BW Yes, it's lewd, isn't it? Octopuses and squid; they're like some counterpoint world to us. That leads quite neatly into the next section – the aquarium-type corridor – because there's something attractive and repulsive about looking into an aquarium. It's nice to put your face right up to the fish, but imagine them actually on your face!

LJ The corridor also mimics the dioramas of a natural history museum. Dioramas are very uncanny, especially those with taxidermy – you're looking at this vivid, often idyllic scene, but everything is dead. With your own surreal dioramas, you also seem to be commenting on the obsessive archiving of objects for museum displays.

BW I'm obsessed with that stuff. When I did a residency at St Fagans [Natural History Museum, Cardiff] in 2008, I really enjoyed going through the whole section in the back: a hundred walking sticks, really scary old hairdressing equipment from the Welsh valleys from the '60s, more harps than you can shake a stick at. And the dioramas that you see in museums – some of them are just fantasy.

LJ   Do you think that *The Gulch* is a bit like walking through a series of life-size dioramas? There are moments where we come very close to the fabric of the installation and we realise that it's fake, whereas from a distance it seems like an incredibly alluring illusion that we could walk into.

BW   I felt like that when I went to see pantomimes as a child. I always thought that it wasn't fair that the audience didn't get to walk through the doorways in the castle or in the backdrop. It's all for the performers. I like allowing the viewer to walk through it all.

LJ   You're allowing us to walk on stage, to take on a performative role.

BW   Yes, that's a really good way of putting it.

LJ   After leaving the corridor we enter a backstage area with some abandoned drums and a drinks vending machine. We have previously talked a lot about the Curve as the backstage space behind the Barbican's Concert Hall, and you're playing with the idea of being behind-the-scenes here.

BW   That's the section most influenced by the Barbican. The glow coming from the drinks machine against that concrete pillar is very 'arts centre', and you often see people playing instruments in the foyer of an arts centre. Oh, I would never take part in a drumming workshop! There's something about that 'come and have a go' thing that as a shy person I don't like; my performances are partly battles with my own shyness.

LJ   It's interesting that you're asking people to get on stage and play the role that you would never play. At many points in *The Gulch* there's the sense that someone's just left the room or the action has just ended; you're in the aftermath of something.

BW   I really like seeing things that summon: 'This book belonged to someone' or 'Somebody just did a spell here'. You're in the wake of somebody's presence. When you're walking in a procession in a museum – and it's the same in Ikea as well – you wonder about the people who've been just before you. And then where the microphone is later on [in the exhibition], if I see somebody ahead of me trying it out, I'll look at them and think 'I'm not going to do that', but maybe later I will. It's very British – we're always very polite walking around exhibits.

LJ   In the next section, you set up a brilliant contrast between the incredibly clinical, corporate conference room and the trippy, psychedelic journey of the film *Flexure* (2016; pp.8–9), in which a depressed hypnotherapist gets hooked on his own hypnotherapy tapes.

BW   I want those things to be very oil and water with each other. I once worked at [what was then called] the Ministry of Agriculture, Fisheries and Food, where I set up conference rooms as a porter. That conference décor, the little sachets of tea and coffee by the urn, the slightly patriarchal vibe, the low level flirting – it's an uncomfortable environment for me.

LJ   I think a lot of people will be able to identify with that. I'm sure many of us have sat in a boardroom and found ourselves going off into a reverie.

BW   Yes. And a lot of companies do yoga and mindfulness in the workplace now, but it's actually to increase productivity. When you go on a course like that, it's like going on the holodeck in Star

Trek: you're disappearing from the real world for a moment. The idea I had at the back of my mind when I was recording the audio for *Flexure* is that it's a journey. I say: 'And now you find yourself in a long corridor, which sweeps away in front of you in a long gentle curve, so that you can see the end of it.' That was from a script that I just copied off the internet but I've changed it – he originally said: 'so that you can't see the end of it.' I thought that if you say 'you can see the end of it', then it's slightly wrong, which makes it trippier.

LJ   In some ways the whole installation feels like we're entering your version of a hypnotherapy tape, it's as if we're going inside your head and you're taking us into a weird altered state. You're the puppet master, rearranging life as we know it.

BW   Hypnotists can go on complete flights of fancy without having to worry about logic and I think that's quite similar to the kind of performance that I do. Actually all the situations in *The Gulch* could easily be hypnotherapy sessions: 'You're on an athletics track...', 'You're in a conference room...' They're situations that make you feel a certain way. Beach: relaxing and mysterious; backstage: not sure exactly where you are; and then the gulch is this quest.

LJ   It's a gulch within a gulch – the Curve itself
      is like a ravine or valley.

BW   Yes, I wanted to explore the idea of somebody
      being small in a crevasse or between two rocks.
      The landscape in areas like the Ogwen Valley in
      Wales is like that. As a tall person, I quite like
      to feel small. I was driving through the Alps
      once and we stopped at a service station and
      I remember just being absolutely wowed by
      the mountain. For me, mountains are things to
      stand next to not to be on top of. The view from
      the top is great, but they're such amazing things
      from below. Scale has been an obsession of
      mine since I was a child.

LJ   There's a talking goat in the gulch section too.
      We've previously talked about the goat as
      Welsh icon, as a tool to satirise the Welsh.

BW   The goat is almost like a Beckett thing, like a troll
      on a bridge, some kind of argumentative, contrary
      or bothersome character. And The Royal Welch
      Fusiliers [now part of The Royal Welsh] even
      have a regimental goat within their ranks! Goats
      are smart but not in an attractive way. They look
      like bad news, don't they? They're slightly un-
      canny, sinister, weird, other, creepy. And a goat's
      voice is strangely at a similar pitch to a human's.

LJ   After hearing the goat speak or perhaps even
      sing, we realise that we can become the source
      of its utterance – the microphone that we find
      upon emerging from the ravine transmits
      directly to the goat's mouth. We can reclaim
      the Curve as a stage for performance, but
      crucially at a remove. There's an element of
      the confessional.

BW   It's like shouting into the reeds. You could feel
      self-conscious walking into the conference room
      but ten minutes later you could be shouting
      nonsense out of the goat's mouth. Giving some-
      one the opportunity to do something that
      appears somewhere else frees them.

LJ   The glitter curtain that separates this section
      from the next provides a lovely backdrop, almost
      like a cabaret theatre. You feel as if you're about
      to step off the stage but you step onto yet
      another: the running track. You're thrust into
      it almost like a competition.

BW   The track follows the natural shape of the Curve.
      It'll be interesting to see whether people will
      rush that last bit. I thought about adding hurdles
      but then I thought that's probably a health and
      safety nightmare!

LJ   Finally we encounter another singing running shoe, this time emitting a male voice. Do you think visitors will be reminded of the single female shoe on the beach and find some kind of resolution?

BW   There's a sense of resolution but it's also quite sad. We feel like we know them both now, but they're not actually together.

LJ   I like the idea that you might be running down the track and you could be distracted by the dulcet tones of the shoe singing to you, which draws you out of the race.

BW   I've always loved putting speakers in things. When we were little, my brother and I used to hide speakers in the garden and goad kids from the other side of the fence! I love this stuff, slightly for its kitsch value, but also for the theatricality of making things appear to be real that aren't.

LJ   We've talked about sound and music quite a lot while working together. You play with oral traditions of storytelling and there are often aural elements in your installations. Is music a trigger for you?

BW   A Welsh hymn played in the background of my performance *Methodist to My Madness* (2008);

even though it's quite a jokey performance,
I wanted the music to be affecting. I figured in a
way that the first 'performance artist' I ever saw
was a preacher, because of the way they modul-
ate their voice to create drama. They're reading
more or less, and it's pretty much how I perform
as well. As a student, I made this sarcastic little
film (*Utility Trousers*, 1999) about trousers that
are unzippable, which included music from Arvo
Pärt's *Spiegel Im Spiegel* (1978). You get this
slow-motion visual of a guy in those trousers set
to the soundtrack.

LJ   It sounds very poignant.

BW   It is! A German guy on my course – we didn't
get on very well – would come into my studio
and patronise me. But then he saw this and said,
'What's great is that I don't know whether to
laugh or cry!'

LJ   I feel like that about a lot of your work! [*laughing*]

BW   I like things that have an emotional pull. It's like
getting two folk singers to do the voices for the
trainers – you listen to it and think it's beautiful,
rather than funny.

LJ   We are mesmerised by them.

BW Yes, that's it: mixing things that are quite amusing and poignant at the same time. Like the German said, 'I don't know whether to laugh or cry.'

1   See Martin Esslin, *The Theatre of the Absurd*, Anchor Books, New York, NY, 1961.

Published in 2016
by Barbican

on the occasion of
Bedwyr Williams: The Gulch
29 September 2016 – 8 January 2017

The Curve
Barbican Centre
Silk Street
London EC2Y 8DS
United Kingdom
barbican.org.uk

Head of Visual Arts: Jane Alison
Assistant Curator: Lotte Johnson
Exhibition Assistant: Luke Naessens

Images © Bedwyr Williams, courtesy
the artist, unless noted otherwise
Texts © the authors
Official copyright for the book © 2016
Barbican Centre, City of London

Copyedited by Daniel Griffiths
Designed and produced by Zak Group
Set in Folio BT
Printed in Belgium by Graphius /
Deckers & Snoeck

ISBN 978 0 952734 16 1

Acknowledgements

Special thanks to Bedwyr Williams, as well as Ann Berni, Tom Bosworth, Vanessa Cass, Camilla Clarke, Max Colson, Katrina Crookall, Kate Davis, Claire Feeley, Ashley Fernandez, Gwyneth Glyn, Claire Jackson, Ewan Jones Morris, Hywel Jones, Patrick Joseph, Sidd Khajuria, Zak Kyes, Chloe Lamford, Margaret Liley, Rebecca May Marston, Twm Morys, Ariane Oiticica, Sally O'Reilly, Barnie Page, Vanessa Pike, Lana Rake-Lasmane, Casey Raymond, Kate Robertson, Robin Scholz, Sunny Smith, Rebecca Spall, Bruce Stracy, Peter Sutton, Andrew Wrenn, Aled Wyn Jones, Lydia Yee and the staff at Barnaby Festival.

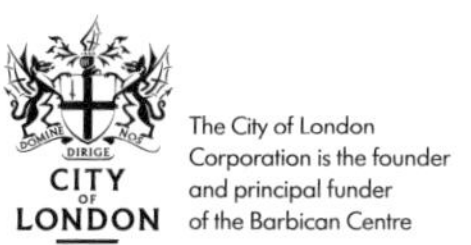

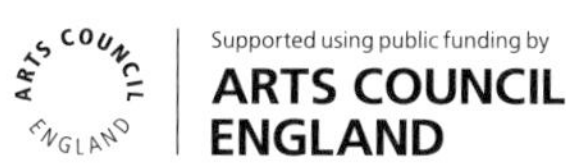

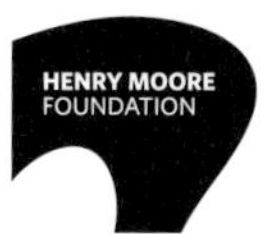

Author Biographies

Sally O'Reilly is a writer, artist, teacher and editor. Recent projects include the novel *Crude* (2016), the libretto for *The Virtues of Things* (2015) and a monograph on Mark Wallinger (2015). She was previously co-editor of *Implicasphere* (2003–08) and author of *The Body in Contemporary Art* (2009). She is currently writer-in-residence at Modern Art Oxford.

Lotte Johnson is Assistant Curator at Barbican Art Gallery, London. Prior to joining the Barbican, she worked at The Museum of Modern Art, New York. The critically acclaimed exhibitions and publications that she has been involved with include *The World of Charles and Ray Eames* (2015); *Roman Signer: Slow Movement* (2015); *Gauguin: Metamorphoses* (2014); *Jasper Johns: Regrets* (2014); *Wait, Later This Will Be Nothing: Editions by Dieter Roth* (2013); and *Printin'* (2012).